INTERVIEW WITH AN Angel

by
Stevan J. Thayer
Linda Sue Nathanson, Ph.D.

Illustrations
Paul W. McCormack

Edin Books, Inc.
Gillette, NJ

The Heart of Interview with an Angel

Edin Books, Inc.
P. O. Box 59
Gillette, New Jersey 07933
908-MIS-EDIN ◆ 908-647-3346

Cover design: Dunn+Associates
Editor: Paula Sirois
Typesetting: Jim Richards

Printed in the United States of America

Photo credits:
    Page 44 – courtesy of National Space Science Data
        Center and the Apollo imaging data suppliers:
        Dr. Frederick J. Doyle, Dr. Richard J. Allenby, Jr.
        and Dr. Farouk El-Baz.
    Pages 36 and 48-49 – Images © 1996 PhotoDisc, Inc.

Library of Congress Cataloging-in-Publication Data

Ariel (Spirit)
        [Interview with an angel. Selections]
        The heart of Interview with an angel / [chan-
    neled] by Stevan J. Thayer ; [interviewed by] Linda
    Sue Nathanson ; illustrations, Paul W. McCormack.
            p.   cm.
        Includes index.
        ISBN 1-887010-05-X (alk. paper)
        1. Spirit writings. I. Thayer, Stevan J. (Stevan
    John), 1950-   . II. Nathanson, Linda Sue.
    III. Title.
        [BF1301.A6172 1997]   97-36017
        133.9'3--dc21   CIP

PROLOGUE

Some say that everyday experiences of intuition and insight, sudden knowing, heightened awareness, dreams, and what we call *coincidence* are all moments when we are being guided by a divine presence. For Stevan J. Thayer, a former electrical engineer, the ordinary suddenly became extraordinary when he began receiving extensive messages from an inner voice identifying itself as an angel named *Ariel*.

Research psychologist Dr. Linda Sue Nathanson – a self-described nonreligious nonbeliever – received Ariel's guidance and healing energy through Stevan. Inspired by a recovery that traditional medicine was unable to explain, Linda initiated a dynamic dialog with Ariel that began with the following question and answer:

Linda: I would like to ask you questions the way an explorer meeting an unknown life form would ask. How do you feel about that?

Ariel: We find it humorous that you would ask us if we would be willing to do what it is that we chose *you* to do.

At the beginning of this extraordinary, two-year, human/angel interview, Ariel said to Linda:

Ariel: We can tell from your questions and the activity of your mind that you have started to understand the reason you and Stevan were selected to work with us. Make no mistake that you two are a force that will guide the revelation of our words to people who are hungry to hear and hungry to read them.

If we could literally move inside of this being you call Stevan and speak directly in a way that could be heard by all, it would be done. But we can trust this treasure, our most precious gift, these words of wisdom to you.

Honoring the trust that Angel Ariel placed in her, Linda formed Edin Books and published *Interview with an Angel* in 1997. *The Heart of Interview with an Angel* is a pocket treasury of Ariel's most powerful, inspiring and thought-provoking messages, drawn from its ground-breaking predecessor. With insights that will ripple through all aspects of your life, this tiny book is an immense gift from the angelic realm to *you* and all humanity — offering the "heart" of an angel's far-reaching views about our world, our selves and our destiny.

A Personal Message from Angel Ariel

*I*t is our fervent desire that all who read these words take them into their hearts; experience them; see how, with free will, the words resonate within their belief system. It is our desire that these words feed and nurture the souls that are hungry for them. *(IWA 95)*

*A*s to the source of our messages — the source is God. *(IWA 126)*

(IWA XX) are page references to
Interview with an Angel.

Angel Ariel Speaks on Angels

*O*ur work begins in this realm with passion that you cannot even imagine. We have an ocean of knowledge, information, poetry, images and wisdom to convey to help the dilemma of your culture and people on your planet. It is our reason for existence — to give this information.

(IWA 333-334)

We speak from a realm that is consciousness, not encumbered by ego and not attached to a physical body. We are souls that have not attached to a physical form. *(IWA 103)*

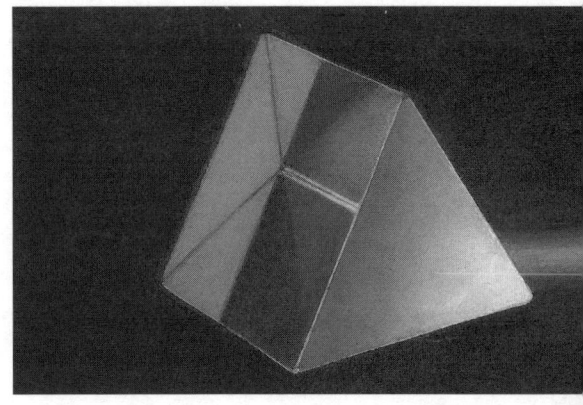

The human mind is like a prism. Since it cannot perceive the entire spectrum at once, it must separate and work on a small section — an infinitesimally small part of what is available in the realm from which we communicate. *(IWA 105-106)*

The various angelic personalities
you perceive are not a reflection of this
realm; they are a reflection of yours.

(IWA 123)

*W*e have worked in many capacities and in many ways with those who can influence an entire race or culture, as well as those who can influence their own lives. Trust in your heart to know that there has been no significant leader — political, religious or in any form throughout time — who has not been touched by the message and by the grace of our work. *(IWA 131)*

♥

Angels Whisper in Your Ear

A thought influenced or sparked by this realm will not just be a mere mental experience. When the thought arises in the mind, it will often have with it a feeling of the heart opening tremendously. *(IWA 120)*

There are so many ways in which we touch and connect to the lives of those we wish to direct, guide and help. While we communicate with humans frequently, their minds often will not acknowledge the origin or importance of our communication. *(IWA 114)*

*Y*ou're at a point in what you call time where, in the not too distant future, it will be an ordinary experience for the vast majority of people to see or to speak with angels. *(IWA 136)*

♥

Angel Ariel Speaks on Love

Love is the substance of this universe. *(IWA 256)*

This realm from which we speak to you is love — nothing more, nothing less. *(IWA 273)*

*T*here is one kind of love, but there are many doors that you can pass through to have that experience. *(IWA 129)*

*T*here's a great deal of love that animals are capable of giving. *(IWA 191)*

*I*t is often the case that people receive more love from animals than they do from other people. The goal would be to find the same degree of affection and the same degree of truth expressed with fellow human beings as you do with animals. *(IWA 300)*

♥

**Angel Ariel Speaks on
Marriage & Divorce**

*M*arriage, as we see it, is what
happens the moment two people see
each other — the moment two souls connect to each other. They bring alive within each other a power, a force that you
tritely call love, but it is far more.

(IWA 140)

When true marriage occurs, there is a power that one soul ignites within the other which allows that soul to come alive. These two souls bring alive the possibility of the fulfillment of each soul's destiny through the very process of their meeting. *(IWA 140)*

*F*rom our realm, marriage can be seen with great ease, for the light that shines forth is very bright. *(IWA 140)*

*D*ivorce, as you see it, is an afterthought. It is first seen from this realm. The light that shines forth from the joining of two souls dims. The power that each person has to support the other in the fulfillment of their lives' and souls' destinies ends. *(IWA 142)*

♥

Angel Ariel Speaks on Fear

Fear is a very personal training ground that each soul must traverse. Drugs and chemicals that attempt to numb fear serve only to temporarily suspend the spiritual training in your life and your soul's journey. Fear must be faced head on and moved through.

(IWA 275)

♥

Angel Ariel Speaks on Good & Evil

*T*here is but one force, one vibration in this universe, and it is the vibration and the force of God. In the human realm, when this vibration is brought openly and freely without distortion into a heart that is ready for it, it produces the most incredible love and what you would call *good.* When pure love from God is brought through a human consciousness filled with fear, that love is distorted into the energy that you call *evil. (IWA 274)*

♥

Angel Ariel Speaks on Illness & Healing

*D*isease can be a warning —

a warning that you are living far from

your truth. *(IWA 166)*

*D*isease can cause a fire to burn

within the very heart of your being such

that your life can be dedicated to the pur-

suit of what you were placed here to do.

(IWA 286)

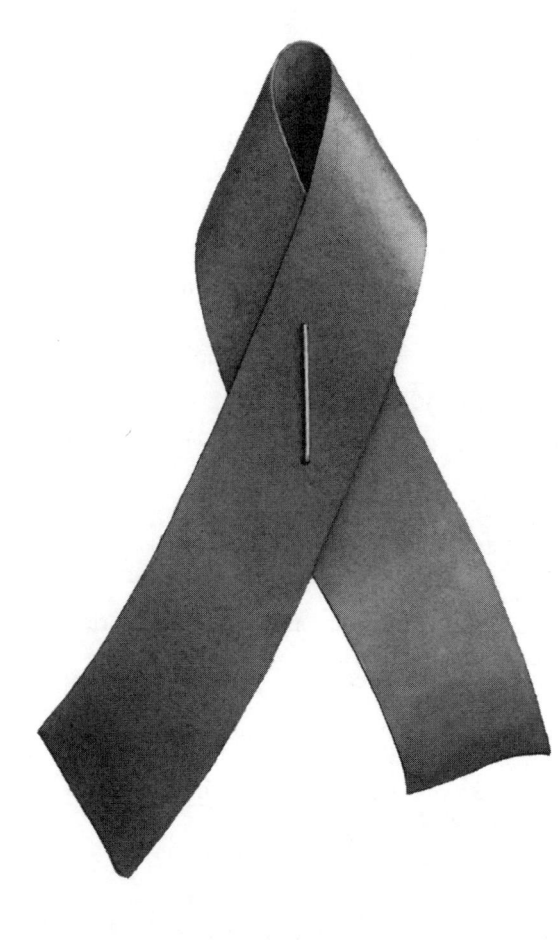

The virus of HIV and the complications and life-threatening consequences known as AIDS are a very personal and direct invitation for every member of the homosexual community, as well as members of the heterosexual community, to wake up to who they truly are and to express that to the world. *(IWA 176)*

*I*t is sometimes the very facing of one's mortality that is the catalyst for the final healing. In these extreme situations, the soul is often pushed to its very edge. It is a time of great inner reflection, often a time of great growth, spiritual union and connection. That soul is never the same again. *(IWA 170)*

♥

Angel Ariel Speaks on Death

*E*ach person who has faced the moment of death knows beyond words, beyond ideas, that it is her time. For she is being invited and beckoned into an ever-increasing level of love that she, from her human perspective, has never experienced. *(IWA 173)*

After the experience of metabolic death, a soul may stay for a period of time around those whom it has much love for and has received much love from. This is often felt by loved ones still abiding within the physical body. This is not a figment of the mind filled with wishful thinking. This is the actual process that transpires as the soul lets go. *(IWA 150)*

*T*he one thing you get to take with you when you leave the physical body is all of the love you have gathered during your life. *(IWA 153)*

♥

Angel Ariel Speaks on Extraterrestrial Life

These beings you call extraterrestrial feel tremendous dismay, having the ability to heal and help fix the wounds, sores and mishaps that humanity faces. They have love to share, shelter to offer and guidance to give as part of the connections you label *abductions.* *(IWA 218)*

*Y*ou ask "How can we extend a
hand of friendship to aliens?" You cannot
even extend a hand of friendship to each
other on your own planet, so it is unrea-
sonable to expect that you could welcome
these life forms that you label as *aliens*.
The truth is that you are not ready.

(IWA 221)

♥

Angel Ariel Speaks on Karma

*E*verything that is experienced in human form is influenced by, a reflection of or a result of karma. *(IWA 178)*

*W*hatever energy you place out into the universe — be it positive or negative, good or bad — will return to you many times over. *(IWA 236)*

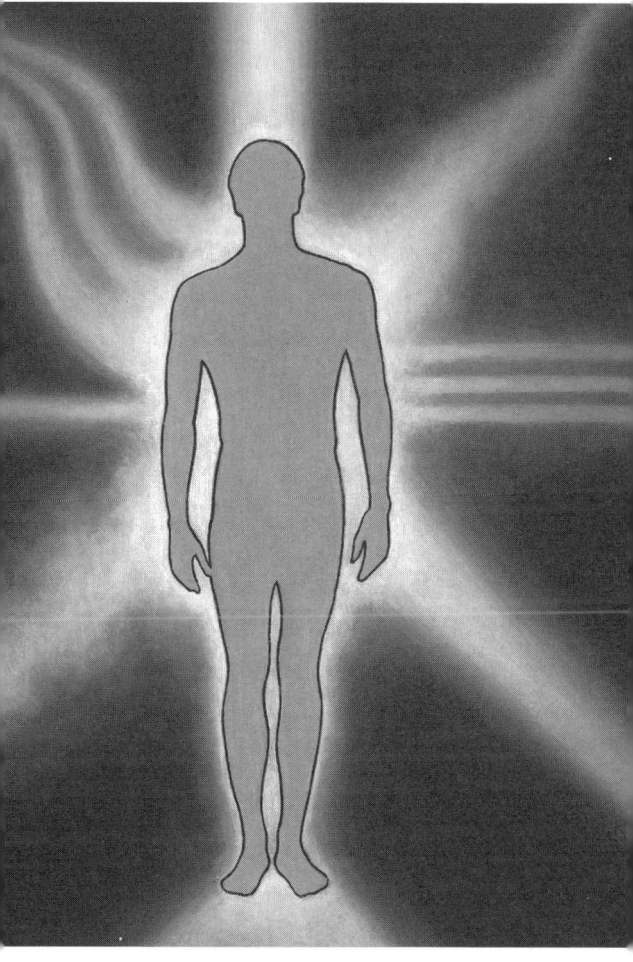

*T*he purpose of karma is not one of punishment. There is no sense of judgment. There is no abiding authority with which to condemn, praise or place any value or judgment whatsoever. Quite simply, each soul grows through the experience that has preceded it. *(IWA 236)*

♥

Angel Ariel Speaks on Religion & God

The method by which one finds the path to meeting God — face-to-face, heart-to-heart, soul-to-soul — is unimportant. The *meeting* is all that matters.

(IWA 208)

The process, path, discipline, religion, teacher, church, synagogue, temple, mosque you choose has very little importance so long as it is the one that nurtures you, teaches you, prods you and propels you toward your goal of knowing God directly. *(IWA 208)*

*I*t is direction from God that is driving your life. Your ego is but a back-seat passenger. *(IWA 264)*

*S*ome people become lost in religion and, as a result, *it* becomes God to them. *(IWA 305)*

*W*hile it is indeed the task within the human mind to move into communion with God, it is also God's love and joy to move into communion with you.

(IWA 132)

♥

Angel Ariel Speaks on Prayer

Prayer should be used constantly, not only in times of need based on fear, which is such a limited use of such a powerful tool. Prayer should be utilized also in times of great joy, fullness and gratitude. *(IWA 210)*

The most powerful form of prayer that you can offer is one in which you pray that the willpower of your own self could be brought into alignment with the will of the universe, the flow of life, or as some have labeled it, the will of God.

(IWA 211)

♥

Angel Ariel Speaks About Our Planet Earth

The Earth is a living being very much as you are a living being. It operates in ways that are only beginning to be understood by the human mind through more advanced scientific observation.

(IWA 181)

*B*e very careful. The planet you are dwelling on is quite capable of defending itself and will defend itself if brought to a point of endangerment. *(IWA 181)*

*E*arth will tolerate only so much destruction. If it comes down to a test between the survival of the Earth and the survival of humans, the Earth will survive. *(IWA 183)*

♥

Angel Ariel Speaks on the Way the Universe Works

*T*hings of the world that might be perceived as setbacks, losses, difficulties or challenges are indeed none other than experiences in the flow of your life that the Divine has lovingly guided you into, to build your strength, redirect your journey, teach you something you will need to know, cause you to meet someone who is important for you to meet or to build an aspect of character that is necessary for what will come. *(IWA 324)*

*I*t is a key spiritual skill for you to develop the ability to learn whether a difficulty is an opportunity for growth or whether it is a signal of misdirection.

(IWA 259)

*Y*ou cannot make one move in life, make one choice, offer one viewpoint, get angry or be happy in a way that does not ripple through and affect the entire structure of your universe. *(IWA 299)*

From the human vantage point, life might seem to be purely arbitrary, random and chaotic with billions of people living in isolation from each other. What you do not see is how each piece is inter-linked with every other piece in perfect harmony. *(IWA 299)*

*I*t is a most frustrating aspect of your human journey to have all the wisdom and the knowledge in front of you, but based on your level of spiritual understanding, to be blind to it. And yet, while the mind is blind, the soul is not. In time, if you are fortunate, the part of you that has gained what you call knowledge will understand what the soul already knows. *(IWA 320)*

*N*othing is by accident.

(IWA 180)

♥

Angel Ariel Speaks on Finding Your Life Purpose

The very thing that you love the most, the very thing that would make you so excited and so happy that it would seem too good to be true, is the very thing that the Divine has for you to do within this life. *(IWA 145-146)*

*T*he human challenge is to read the heart's compass and find what it points to.

(IWA 146)

*I*f it is important that you be used in service to the Divine, you will be filled with everything you need to carry out the tasks. *(IWA 133)*

Prosperity is measured in love, wealth, health, well-being, joy, harmony and enthusiasm. The path to your highest prosperity is to follow your heart and live your dream. *(IWA 330)*

The force of the universe that exists on your planet has never been as powerful or as strong as it is at this moment in time. This is a time to call forth, to face the fears, to face the internal challenges and dare to be what you were designed and created to be.

(IWA 330)

♥ ♥ ♥

INDEX

Stevan J. Thayer

Stevan J. Thayer, a former electrical engineer who became an interfaith minister following a profound mystical experience, serves as a voice of Angel Ariel's loving wisdom and healing energy. A nationally televised speaker, Stevan conducts Healing with the Energy of Angels® workshops and has developed and teaches an energy therapy approach called Integrated Energy Therapy.® Stevan received a Master of Science in Electrical Engineering from Columbia University and was ordained by the New Seminary in New York. Stevan lives with his wife Carol in New Jersey.

Linda Sue Nathanson

Trained as a research psychologist, Linda Sue Nathanson earned her Ph.D. from the University of California, Los Angeles (UCLA). She was twice a National Science Foundation Summer Research Fellow, was a research fellow at UCLA, and held a post-doctoral research fellowship at the Albert Einstein College of Medicine. Linda is listed in six national and international *Who's Who* directories. Now a writer, speaker and publisher, Linda lives in New Jersey with her husband and feline family.

ORDER FORM

EDIN BOOKS *Inc.*

More of Ariel's wisdom is available from Edin Books.

Sold To:

NAME _____

ORDER DATE _____

ADDRESS _____

ADDRESS (CONT.) _____

SUITE / APARTMENT # _____

CITY _____

STATE _____

ZIP _____

COUNTRY _____

Ship To: if different from **Sold To:**

NAME _____

ADDRESS _____

ADDRESS (CONT.) _____

SUITE / APARTMENT # _____

CITY _____

STATE _____

ZIP _____

COUNTRY _____

Merchandise Ordered

PRODUCT DESCRIPTION	QUANTITY	UNIT PRICE	TOTAL
Interview with an Angel *Softcover, 368 pages*		$16.95	$
Interview with an Angel Hardcover, 368 pages		$24.95	$
"Ask an Angel" newsletter – 10 issues Ariel answers readers' questions		$29.95	$
The Heart of Interview with an Angel Softcover, 64 pages		$4.95	$
Healing with the Energy of Angels (AUDIO) Workshop by Stevan Thayer – 4 tapes		$29.95	$
		Subtotal	$
		6% Sales Tax IN NEW JERSEY	$
		Shipping • $3 for first item	$
		• Add'l items _____ x $1 ea.	$
		• Orders outside U.S. add $10	$
		TOTAL	$

Method of Payment

☐ Check, payable to *Edin Books* in US dollars

☐ Money order   ☐ MasterCard

☐ VISA   ☐ Amer. Express

CARD NO _____ EXP DATE _____

SIGNATURE _____

PHONE (_____) _____ ☐ Day ☐ Evening

908 · 580 · 1008
24 hours a day

Edin Books
P.O. Box 59
Gillette, NJ 07933

EdinBooks
@aol.com

1 · 800 · 334 · 6477
(US only)
908 · MIS · EDIN
(908 · 647 · 3346)
9 am - 9 pm Eastern

An Angel Invites Your Questions

In *Interview with an Angel (IWA)*, an angel named Ariel answered 153 questions. Now, you can ask Ariel your own questions, **FREE**.

> *"Those burning questions that come from the soul are ones we seek, for those are the ones through which we can most effectively do our work.*
>
> *Those that question things that have less global bearing provide less of a forum within which we can work. Please do not ask us for what you should do. Ask us, instead, how we interpret or how we explain a phenomenon."* (IWA 326)

Angel Ariel

Send your questions by mail, fax or email. Selected questions and answers will appear in the syndicated column **"Ask an Angel"** *and in future publications.*

Don't miss a message! Subscribe to **"Ask an Angel"** *newsletter and receive* **all** *of Angel Ariel's life-changing wisdom.*

See previous page for contact information and Order Form. Questions become the property of Edin Books and may be edited for clarity, grammar or length. Names and addresses remain strictly confidential and will not be published.